365 Erotic Reasons Why I Love You

Asa Leveaux

Phoenix Ink
New York

365 EROTIC REASONS WHY I LOVE YOU
© Copyright Asa Leveaux.
All Rights Reserved.

© Copyright Asa Leveaux. All Rights Reserved. This publication is provided subject to the condition that it shall not, by way of trade or otherwise, be lent, resold, hired out or otherwise circulated without the author's prior written consent in any form of binding or cover. No part of this publication may be reproduced by any process, nor may it be stored in a retrieval system, transmitted or otherwise copied for public or private use without the written permission of the author. Although the author has made every reasonable attempt to achieve complete accuracy of the content in this article, they assume no responsibility for errors or omissions. Use the information in this article at your own risk. Any trademarks, service marks, product names or named features are assumed to be the property of their respective owners, and are used only for reference. There is no implied endorsement if we use one of these terms.

DEDICATION

This book is dedicated to my lover and friend, Alexis. You are the inspiration for this project, the intensity behind the words and the joy in the reasons.

These 365 Erotic Reasons are dedicated to:

_____

From Your:

_____

_____

_____

Foreword

Welcome to *365 Erotic Reasons Why I Love You*. My intent is that you find your way back to your partner's heart and in doing so have your heart and your pants set ablaze with passion. Whether your love has just begun, if you have the war wounds of many moons, if in an interracial relationship or if you believe that no one can please you like someone with the same equipment as your own, this will serve as co-dependent guide. This guide will give you an electric shock to propel you and your lover to further mutual love, respect, intimacy and sessions that will leave you panting, or even begging, not to end. Throughout the book, you will find that you can add to the pages to make it personalized. For instance, once you reach the day that gives the reason of how quick trips become road trips, you and your partner can think of times this has happened, leading to further appreciation. An example of how to do this would be including how you love the way they ask for directions when they are lost, which would allow them to respond how they appreciate you ensuring that their car and body

are always filled with the fuel it needs. As your relationship is dependent upon your participation, so is this guide. Anticipate the next 365 days being complete with appreciation, love and a level of eroticism that you can create and consume.

Day 1: The way your lips part

Me:

_____

_____

You:

_____

_____

Day 2: How you swallow confidently

Me:

―――――――――――――――

―――――――――――――――

You:

―――――――――――――――

―――――――――――――――

Day 3: The way you look in nothing at all

Me:
_____

_____

You:
_____

_____

Day 4: Choosing to undress me with your teeth instead of your eyes

Me:

_____

_____

You:

_____

_____

Day 5: The shape of your body

Me:

You:

Day 6: The way you allow me to ravish you

Me:

_____

_____

You:

_____

_____

Day 7: The way our bodies fit naturally; crevice to crevice

Me:

You:

Day 8: Having you for breakfast

Me:

———————————————

———————————————

You:

———————————————

———————————————

Day 9: When you allow my tongue to connect the dots

Me:

_____

_____

You:

_____

_____

Day 10: The look that lets me know its all mine

Me:

———————————————

———————————————

You:

———————————————

———————————————

Day 11: The way you blush when I touch you in public

Me:

You:

Day 12: The way you arouse me without being near me

Me:
_____
_____

You:
_____
_____

Day 13: How I know it's all mine before I ask

Me:

_____

_____

You:

_____

_____

Day 14: When you tell me what

Me:

You:

Day 15: The way you whisper softly to me

Me:

You:

Day 16: How your body makes me fall in love again and again

Me:

You:

Day 17: The way honey accentuates your taste

Me:

You:

Day 18: The way your body feels under my hands

Me:
_____
_____

You:
_____
_____

Day 19: You are the sole reason for my blood flow to be re-routed

Me:

You:

365 Erotic Reasons Why I Love You

Day 20: The number of awards you have won for starring in my wet dreams

Me:

———————————
———————————

You:

———————————
———————————

Day 21: The way you rub the waves and curls out of my head when I feast on you

Me:

You:

365 Erotic Reasons Why I Love You

Day 22: The way you offer your ass when I'm behind you

Me:

_____

_____

You:

_____

_____

Day 23: The way you effortlessly change positions

Me:

You:

Day 24: The way you make my body tingle at the thought of you

Me:

You:

Day 25: Succumbing to my desire to feel you before dawn

Me:

You:

Day 26: Seeing the vision of your form from the back

Me:

You:

Day 27: Introducing me to internal peaks and valleys

Me:

_____

_____

You:

_____

_____

Day 28: Awakening the arousal that was dormant within me

Me:

You:

Day 29: Watching you watching me shower in preparation

Me:

You:

Day 30: You allow me to master my oral fixation with your flesh

Me:

You:

Day 31: The way quick trips become road trips

Me:

You:

Day 32: You allowing my mouth to finish what my hands have started

Me:

You:

Day 33: The way we argue just so that we can properly make up...in sweat

Me:

You:

Day 34: When you proclaimed my face to be your royal throne

Me:

You:

Day 35: Your combination of sadistic sensitivity

Me:

You:

Day 36: The hypnotizing rhythm of your moan

Me:
_____
_____

You:
_____
_____

Day 37: When I say don't stop you know it's merely a suggestion

Me:

You:

Day 38: You allow me to manipulate your limbs in ways that are purely imaginative

Me:

You:

Day 39: The way you accept my erotic challenge with a grin

Me:

_____

_____

You:

_____

_____

Day 40: How your feet in the air are a vision from heaven

Me:

You:

Day 41: The delightful way you render my comfort zone useless

Me:

_____

_____

You:

_____

_____

Day 42: How with us routine showering becomes anything but routine

Me:

You:

Day 43: When the climax can only happen by looking into your eyes

Me:

You:

Day 44: The way you've made going faster change from the standard to an option

Me:

You:

Day 45: How a standing ovation begins when we are alone

Me:
_____

_____

You:
_____

_____

Day 46: The way you place my needs and wants before your own

Me:

You:

Day 47: Nowadays touching you is no longer a daydream but rather a nightly reality

Me:

You:

Day 48: How passion infused ecstasy and kisses have become gourmet meals

Me:

You:

Day 49: The way you have my body constructed into various amusement parks

Me:

You:

Day 50: You have made the word "magic" a better description of what we are capable of

Me:

You:

Day 51: The way your curves, tilts, and lines have convinced my fingers that video games are now obsolete

Me:

———————————————

———————————————

You:

———————————————

———————————————

Day 52: The night you transformed from candy to soul food

Me:

You:

Day 53: How the words your brain composes sends my body into throbbing waves

Me:

You:

365 Erotic Reasons Why I Love You

Day 54: We don't need oceans for our bodies to rock on waves of excitement

Me:

You:

Day 55: You have made my lips, skin and deltoids your daily supply of LSD

Me:

You:

Day 56: How you don't want to make me scream since intense silence is your goal

Me:

You:

Day 57: The intensity of your lovemaking that makes me reach for air that isn't there

Me:

You:

Day 58: When you have more juices than diced pineapples

Me:

You:

Day 59: The way you've made our bed an archaeological site with the times your body parts have been buried in the mattress

Me:

You:

Day 60: How I am just as intrigued by our first escapade as our next one

Me:

You:

Day 61: How even though you can't swim you've won medals for your stroke

Me:

You:

Day 62: The shape of your lips

Me:

You:

365 Erotic Reasons Why I Love You

Day 63: Watching us in playback mode excites you for the next scene

Me:

You:

Day 64: The text I receive at noon suggesting that I begin stretching

Me:

You:

Day 65: The way you grab my hips as you search for my soul

Me:

You:

Day 66: You're capable of making me finish before I get started

Me:

_____

_____

You:

_____

_____

Day 67: How the dichotomy of your sensuality can touch both body and soul

Me:

You:

Day 68: The way your hands make my body speak in tongues when baptized in you

Me:

You:

Day 69: The way we have mastered this number

Me:

You:

Day 70: Watching you walk into a room

Me:

———

———

You:

———

———

Day 71: Watching you walk across a room

Me:

You:

Day 72: Watching you walk out of the room

Me:

You:

Day 73: How your tongue will speak body languages

Me:

You:

Day 74: That moment right before...

Me:

You:

Day 75: Because no one else has ever put a bruise there

Me:

You:

365 Erotic Reasons Why I Love You

Day 76: How you can bring thunder, lightning and rain to a bedroom

Me:

You:

Day 77: The way you allow shoulder blades to embrace cold walls

Me:

You:

365 Erotic Reasons Why I Love You

Day 78: The way you bite your lips and I know just what to prescribe

Me:

You:

Day 79: You've agreed to let me show you the difference between lust and intimacy

Me:

You:

Day 80: when you choose to allow the headboard to talk for you

Me:

———————————

———————————

You:

———————————

———————————

Day 81: You tell people that I am the best part of waking up

Me:

You:

365 Erotic Reasons Why I Love You

Day 82: You'd rather stay connected as the swelling goes down

Me:

You:

Day 83: When you call me a pink fiend

Me:

You:

Day 84: The way you paint on my canvas with detail and passion

Me:

———————————————

———————————————

You:

———————————————

———————————————

Day 85: The way the chains reflect off your eyes

Me:

You:

365 Erotic Reasons Why I Love You

Day 86: You trust me to massage your body into a state of delusion

Me:

You:

Day 87: You'd rather tear my clothes than break your promises

Me:

You:

Day 88: Now I buy spices and condiments based on how I think they will taste on you

Me:

_____

_____

You:

_____

_____

Day 89: The way your toes curl like permed hair

Me:

_____

_____

You:

_____

_____

Day 90: The way you watch me devour a meal and to know that you're next

Me:

You:

Day 91: How your holds become grasps that become pinches that go free

Me:

You:

Day 92: Because you've made me realize that I've been doing yoga for years

Me:

You:

Day 93: The beautiful way you touch yourself when you see me

Me:

You:

Day 94: The way we have mastered grinding to the beat of musical syncopations

Me:

―――――――――――

―――――――――――

You:

―――――――――――

―――――――――――

Day 95: Your pillows can assist in conquests and confessionals

Me:

You:

Day 96: I now know that the pot of gold is not really at the end of the rainbow

Me:

You:

Day 97: After that I now can't remember my last lover's name

Me:

You:

365 Erotic Reasons Why I Love You

Day 98: Sometimes you in those jeans make me forget my own name

Me:

———————————————

———————————————

You:

———————————————

———————————————

Day 99: Before you midnight was nap time and now it has become recess

Me:

_____

_____

You:

_____

_____

Day 100: The only proper description of you is!!!!!!!!!!!!!!!!!!!!!!!!!

Me:

You:

---

365 Erotic Reasons Why I Love You

Day 101: Instead of cheating you focus on finding new ways to show how much you love me

Me:

You:

Day 102: The way you say thank you gives me the motivation to do more

Me:

You:

Day 103: You don't have to brag with the way you make my body sing in minor octaves

Me:

You:

Day 104: We both know how to make foreplay the main course

Me:

You:

Day 105: You've mastered the touch on how to make me hang up the phone

Me:

You:

Day 106: Now there is not a reason for me to ever say "I've never done that before"

Me:
_____
_____

You:
_____
_____

Day 107: The neighbors know our names though we've never been invited over

Me:

You:

---

365 Erotic Reasons Why I Love You

Day 108: Now countertops and staircases are symbolisms of us

Me:

You:

Day 109: You, at times, give me a case of tourettes

Me:

You:

Day 110: Now hair pulling is one of my favorite past times

Me:

You:

Day 111: When you say that I am the only one that can make you do that more than once

Me:

You:

Day 112: You've shown me that I don't necessarily have to breathe properly to have an amazing time

Me:

You:

Day 113: I know I can wake up to you massaging my feet after work

Me:

You:

Day 114: No one else understands the way we know how to combine gymnastics and a monster truck show in a kitchen

Me:

You:

Day 115: The way you smile at me from across the room

Me:

You:

365 Erotic Reasons Why I Love You

Day 116: You've allowed me to discover just how many licks it takes to get to the center

Me:

You:

Day 117: I never knew that someone could place their lips there, but I do now

Me:

You:

Day 118: You know how to wrap your arms around me to make the pain go away

Me:

You:

Day 119: I find myself smiling at the office about the night before and the days to come

Me:

You:

Day 120: You've finally realized that I need you in my life

Me:

You:

Day 121: You have a degree in what turns me on, with honors

Me:

You:

365 Erotic Reasons Why I Love You

Day 122: I never knew it was possible for someone's body to move like that before yesterday

Me:

———————————

———————————

You:

———————————

———————————

Day 123: You aren't afraid to show me your deepest fears

Me:

_____

_____

You:

_____

_____

Day 124: The way you giggle when I tell you that you are better than my mom's peach cobbler

Me:

You:

Day 125: The way you have defined love in a new and exciting way

Me:

You:

Day 126: The way you...just...keep...going

Me:

———————————————

———————————————

You:

———————————————

———————————————

Day 127: How you enter my sanctuary and fall on your knees to do everything but pray

Me:

You:

Day 128: How you're there for me before I can request you

Me:

You:

365 Erotic Reasons Why I Love You

Day 129: I just can't stay away from you too long

Me:

_____

_____

You:

_____

_____

365 Erotic Reasons Why I Love You

Day 130: You've made the fantasies that I've searched for available and made to order

Me:

You:

Day 131: When you refer to my body as the land of milk and honey

Me:

You:

365 Erotic Reasons Why I Love You

Day 132: How you've made my thoughts become things

Me:

You:

Day 133: I feel the passion in your touch, in your duties and in your words

Me:

You:

Day 134: The way your eyes transport me into an exotic abyss effortlessly

Me:

You:

Day 135: The way arches no longer make my mouth water for fries

Me:

You:

---

365 Erotic Reasons Why I Love You

Day 136: You know there is more to love than a climatic experience

Me:

You:

Day 137: The note you left in my pocket that said "I am meant for your indulgence"

Me:

You:

365 Erotic Reasons Why I Love You

Day 138: Watching your toes point as if they are reaching through eternity

Me:

You:

Day 139: Because you catch me every time I fall

Me:

You:

365 Erotic Reasons Why I Love You

Day 140: Because you are so satisfying that I don't need to eat once I've had you

Me:

You:

Day 141: Kissing the ample moist part of your lips

Me:

_____

_____

You:

_____

_____

Day 142: You have believed in me when there was no one left

Me:

You:

Day 143: You have made me look at automobiles in a new and vibrant way

Me:

You:

Day 144: You aren't scared about what's coming next

Me:
_____

_____

You:
_____

_____

Day 145: The way you look back at me

Me:

You:

Day 146: I never have to beg for it even though it's worth it

Me:

You:

Day 147: The way you have quenched my appetite for all things edible and for some that aren't

Me:

You:

Day 148: The way your patience has removed the callous on my heart

Me:

You:

Day 149: You don't mind replacing lamps and mattresses

Me:

You:

Day 150: The way the kids think you are a superhero

Me:
___
___

You:
___
___

Day 151: When you told me that I am the happy ending to your fairy tale

Me:

You:

365 Erotic Reasons Why I Love You

Day 152: You don't judge my thoughts but instead nourish them

Me:

You:

Day 153: The way your adolescent wants have grown into adult needs

Me:

You:

Day 154: That moment when you begin to unbutton your shirt

Me:
_____
_____

You:
_____
_____

Day 155: The way you allow me to dip into you

Me:

_____

_____

You:

_____

_____

Day 156: How our breathing becomes united as our lips separate

Me:

———————————————

———————————————

You:

———————————————

———————————————

Day 157: Those moments when you obey every command

Me:

You:

Day 158: How the sunlight hits your face just the right way

Me:

You:

Day 159: watching you work on one of your many projects with the intensity reserved for me

Me:

You:

365 Erotic Reasons Why I Love You

Day 160: No one has ever made me desire to wish I were a bead of sweat

Me:

You:

365 Erotic Reasons Why I Love You

Day 161: The way your neck bends when you laugh out loud

Me:

You:

Day 162: When you lean across me to tell me I'm beautiful

Me:

You:

Day 163: When you say those 3 sensual words..."I got it"

Me:

You:

Day 164: When you serve me cake in your birthday suit

Me:
_____
_____

You:
_____
_____

Day 165: How your face lights up when you receive my flowers

Me:

You:

Day 166: The way you hold me on the subway

Me:

You:

365 Erotic Reasons Why I Love You

Day 167: You agree that thighs can also serve as earmuffs

Me:

You:

Day 168: The rise and fall of your frame as you workout

Me:

You:

365 Erotic Reasons Why I Love You

Day 169: When you transitioned from friend to family

Me:

You:

Day 170: You've become a vault for all of my secrets

Me:

You:

Day 171: I now know your previous lovers were merely practice

Me:

―――――――――――――――――
―――――――――――――――――

You:

―――――――――――――――――
―――――――――――――――――

Day 172: The way you awakened the love in me and then reciprocated it

Me:

You:

Day 173: The way you do simple things in an extraordinary way

Me:

You:

Day 174: How you let me find myself within you

Me:

You:

Day 175: The way I love to watch how you can command a room without speaking

Me:

You:

365 Erotic Reasons Why I Love You

Day 176: When you still get jealous when someone flirts with me

Me:

You:

Day 177: How you look at me like you're trying to find out just what's under my clothes and if you could tame it

Me:

You:

Day 178: The way every bulge is just where it should be

Me:

You:

365 Erotic Reasons Why I Love You

Day 179: You're hard enough to push my hands away and soft enough to wipe the tears away

Me:

You:

Day 180: The way your silhouette is just as alluring as the real thing

Me:

———————————

———————————

You:

———————————

———————————

Day 181: How your scent evokes memories of body twirls, sweat rhythms, falsetto moans and moist desire

Me:

You:

Day 182: Your hands knowing the contour of my body as though you built it

Me:

You:

Day 183: If I dared to tell anyone what we just did, it would all have to be bleeped out

Me:

You:

Day 184: You've turned the blues of life to a wild tango of bodies entangled in pastries

Me:

You:

Day 185: The amazing thing you do that makes it seem like you're touching all things at once that renders you other than human

Me:

_____

_____

You:

_____

_____

365 Erotic Reasons Why I Love You

Day 186: Holding me

Me:

You:

Day 187: How you teach me the constellations then allow me to make my own on the heavens of you

Me:

You:

Day 188: When you make words superfluous

Me:

You:

Day 189: How I feel like I've been kissed by the wind when you speak to me

Me:

You:

365 Erotic Reasons Why I Love You

Day 190: When you kiss me with the energy of 3 supernovas

Me:

_____

_____

You:

_____

_____

Day 191: You never compare me to those that came before me

Me:

You:

Day 192: I've found that you are a treasure chest of amazing

Me:
_____

_____

You:
_____

_____

Day 193: How your aura makes me lightheaded

Me:

You:

Day 194: The way you can be my master and my personal concierge in the same day

Me:

You:

Day 195: The seduction of your forehead kisses

Me:

You:

Day 196: The times when you don't care who is watching

Me:

You:

Day 197: That picture of yourself you just sent me

Me:

You:

Day 198: When our tickle fights turns to teasing

Me:
_____
_____

You:
_____
_____

Day 199: When I nursed you back to health, you rewarded me with the opportunity to suckle you

Me:

You:

365 Erotic Reasons Why I Love You

Day 200: How you trace the outline of my lips with yours

Me:

You:

Day 201: With you I'd rather be tied up than free

Me:

You:

365 Erotic Reasons Why I Love You

Day 202: Clothes have gone from optional to forbidden

Me:

You:

Day 203: The glimpse of you passing across the doorway excites my sensations

Me:

You:

365 Erotic Reasons Why I Love You

Day 204: When our rings and bodies connect at the same time

Me:

_____

_____

You:

_____

_____

Day 205: The times your discretion leaves and you stay

Me:

You:

---

365 Erotic Reasons Why I Love You

Day 206: Now I know that I don't have to make it alone

Me:
_____
_____

You:
_____
_____

365 Erotic Reasons Why I Love You

Day 207: The reality that I no longer need batteries

Me:
_____

_____

You:
_____

_____

Day 208: When I woke up and discovered a clean house

Me:

You:

Day 209: At nights when you choose me over your laptop

Me:

You:

Day 210: Because you're better than I daydream

Me:
_____

_____

You:
_____

_____

Day 211: When you tell me that I was the reason you smiled all day

Me:

You:

Day 212: You making it so hard to take you straight home

Me:

You:

365 Erotic Reasons Why I Love You

Day 213: How breathless I get when you call my name

Me:

You:

365 Erotic Reasons Why I Love You

Day 214: The way you feel that I must get out of my wet clothes when coming in from the rain

Me:

You:

Day 215: When you tell the waiter that we have decided to have dessert at home.

Me:

_____

_____

You:

_____

_____

Day 216: The tender ritual of you tending to my new bite marks and scratches

Me:
_____

_____

You:
_____

_____

Day 217: The times when you steer my body as though we're going off roading

Me:

You:

Day 218: What's happening under the table is so much more delicious than what's on top

Me:

You:

Day 219: Though I'm about to be sensually violated, I have purposefully forgotten the number to the police

Me:

You:

365 Erotic Reasons Why I Love You

Day 220: You've made trust so much more than a promise of possibility

Me:

You:

Day 221: I now wake up from a dream next to a dream

Me:

You:

Day 222: When you know that I don't need to be strong at that moment

Me:

You:

Day 223: There's not a morsel of you that you deny for my consumption

Me:

You:

Day 224: How you can run your business and still make time for fantasies

Me:

———————————————

———————————————

You:

———————————————

———————————————

Day 225: When we're deep it has little to do with intellect

Me:

_____

_____

You:

_____

_____

Day 226: The days we have picnics we make nature blush at our nature

Me:

You:

Day 227: How you make every part of me leak with adoration

Me:

You:

Day 228: The hugs you give me when your hands are tied

Me:

You:

365 Erotic Reasons Why I Love You

Day 229: I've learned that planking is fun when done well

Me:

You:

Day 230: The masterful way you combine hot wax and ice

Me:

You:

Day 231: How you dare me to take it

Me:

_____

_____

You:

_____

_____

Day 232: You love auditioning for my next full feature film

Me:

You:

365 Erotic Reasons Why I Love You

Day 233: When I realize that you played me like a harmonica while strumming my guitar strings

Me:

You:

365 Erotic Reasons Why I Love You

Day 234: When you accept the invitation to cordially take me

Me:

You:

Day 235: The way you don't try to fix me but rather play in all the various cracks

Me:

You:

Day 236: How you desire to read my mind by Braille, which seems to be a full body book

Me:

———————————————

———————————————

You:

———————————————

———————————————

365 Erotic Reasons Why I Love You

Day 237: You've made biting me an implied task

Me:

_____

_____

You:

_____

_____

Day 238: The kiss you give me after I've turned you into a human origami

Me:

You:

Day 239: How you made the dining room table a stage…and what a performance

Me:

You:

Day 240: Because the rodeos in Oklahoma should come study us

Me:

You:

Day 241: When we bathe the cleaner you get the dirtier I become

Me:

You:

Day 242: The satisfaction you receive from playing with everything except my heart

Me:

You:

Day 243: How you get a little nervous when you realize what's about to happen

Me:

You:

Day 244: The way you succumb to me utilizing, holding, grasping and restraining 3 limbs at once

Me:

You:

Day 245: How you can make my face look exactly as it did on the roller coaster

Me:

You:

365 Erotic Reasons Why I Love You

Day 246: The suggestive way you press up against me at the grocery store

Me:

You:

Day 247: Because you relish in my fetish

Me:

You:

Day 248: The moisture of the mix of sweat and tears creating a pool on me

Me:

You:

Day 249: Because two days after our session we're still uncovering hair and clothing

Me:

You:

365 Erotic Reasons Why I Love You

Day 250: The sexy way you wear the smile I gave you

Me:

You:

Day 251: How our lovemaking is as beautiful as the love

Me:

You:

Day 252: My only regret is not allowing you to touch me sooner

Me:

You:

Day 253: Opening the front door and finding you in the position that takes my breath away

Me:

You:

365 Erotic Reasons Why I Love You

Day 254: How I'm still recovering the morning after with aftershock and morning dew

Me:

You:

365 Erotic Reasons Why I Love You

Day 255: How your ankles and my earlobes have learned to get along so well

Me:

You:

Day 256: The way you get lost in my eyes and don't pay attention to what I'm saying

Me:

You:

Day 257: How my hand fits perfectly into yours

Me:

You:

Day 258: I've learned that I don't need syrup for love to be sticky and sweet although at times I indulge

Me:

You:

Day 259: The way you fill all of my dimples with your kisses

Me:

You:

Day 260: Cause your tongue should be bronzed

Me:

You:

Day 261: I see the value in the price I've paid to hold you

Me:

You:

365 Erotic Reasons Why I Love You

Day 262: I know what Sonia Sanchez meant when she wrote "on our bed each night I breathe you and become high".
Me:

Me:

You:

Day 263: You do it so well that I want to tell everyone. Then I think about that and just tell my dog.

Me:

You:

365 Erotic Reasons Why I Love You

Day 264: This morning I am thankful that you can defy the law of gravity

Me:

You:

Day 265: For your birthday you told me that my presence was the present

Me:

You:

Day 266: Because you can guarantee to return the favor

Me:
_____

_____

You:
_____

_____

Day 267: How having only one of your body parts visible to me that it makes me want to touch you and me at the same time

Me:

You:

Day 268: I've now been conditioned to salivate at the sounds of the shower

Me:

You:

Day 269: How I can get lost in your flavor

Me:

You:

Day 270: Waking up to you watching me sleep

Me:

———————————————

———————————————

You:

———————————————

———————————————

Day 271: When you tell me that I deserve a sandwich after that but you're still waiting for your ability to walk to begin again

Me:

You:

365 Erotic Reasons Why I Love You

Day 272: The way your eyes roll back when I slip and slide back and forth side to side

Me:

_____

_____

You:

_____

_____

Day 273: The geometry lessons you teach me as you lick me in circles with hexagonal force

Me:

You:

Day 274: When you choose to squeeze me until cream takes the place of oxygen

Me:

You:

Day 275: With us there isn't a need to take pictures because it will happen again in 5...4...3...2...1

Me:

You:

365 Erotic Reasons Why I Love You

Day 276: I know every time I move tomorrow I'll be reminded that you were here, here and there.

Me:

You:

Day 277: The times you read my lips like a bible and love my body like a sin

Me:

You:

Day 278: You offering your body up as a wet sacrifice

Me:

_____

_____

You:

_____

_____

Day 279: To tease or not to tease that is the question.

Me:

_____

_____

You:

_____

_____

Day 280: Watching in anticipation the way our shadows become one being on the wall created by candlelight

Me:

You:

Day 281: The power you have to create raindrops in my bed sheets without overcast or cloudy skies

Me:

You:

Day 282: You just told your parents that I'm here to stay

Me:

You:

Day 283: The cadence in which you repeat my name matching the crescendo of my thrusts

Me:

You:

Day 284: Speaking foreign languages in my ear that give me the power to complete you with unknown tongues

Me:

You:

Day 285: Watching how you please yourself

Me:

You:

Day 286: Feeling the heat radiate from your sex in anticipation of harvesting me

Me:

You:

Day 287: The way you part my thighs, play with your food and then attempt to become satisfied with what I have to offer

Me:

You:

Day 288: When I was notified that you had accepted the position to be my whore

Me:

———————————————

———————————————

You:

———————————————

———————————————

365 Erotic Reasons Why I Love You

Day 289: The way you can put your fingers in places that show me your intentions

Me:

You:

Day 290: When I looked out into the audience and saw you smiling

Me:

_____

_____

You:

_____

_____

Day 291: Your success is based on the degree of carpet burns

Me:

You:

365 Erotic Reasons Why I Love You

Day 292: Enjoying you kissing down my spine while you caress up my inner thigh

Me:

You:

Day 293: You said you've spent the last hour trying to find a way to bottle me or put me in pill form

Me:

You:

365 Erotic Reasons Why I Love You

Day 294: Only you know how to lap it all up until there is none left

Me:

You:

Day 295: Though my rotisserie culinary experiment became a Cajun disaster you ate it all the same

Me:

You:

Day 296: We agree that swings are anything but child's play

Me:

You:

Day 297: Turning off the lights has become synonymous with "LET'S GET READY TO RUMBLE!"

Me:

You:

Day 298: My body dangling over your couch is the start of sex therapy

Me:

———————————

———————————

You:

———————————

———————————

Day 299: It's now customary to find my underwear on the ceiling and your skin under my fingernails

Me:

You:

Day 300: Cause I can tell this will not be over quickly

Me:

———————————————

———————————————

You:

———————————————

———————————————

Day 301: Feeling the pulse of your heartbeat as I write my name with my mouth across your body and vibrate exclamation points

Me:

You:

Day 302: The almighty view of watching you please me on your knees

Me:

You:

Day 303: You would rather give than receive

Me:

You:

Day 304: The memory of scoring a touchdown on the 50-yard line at your old high school without a ball

Me:

_____

_____

You:

_____

_____

365 Erotic Reasons Why I Love You

Day 305: Giggling at the fence marks that are still imprinted on your back

Me:

You:

Day 306: We still are able to receive cheers when we perform on the balcony

Me:
_____
_____

You:
_____
_____

Day 307: Knowing that the next time I catch you in the laundry room you can expect your body to be rinsed on high and then repeated

Me:

You:

365 Erotic Reasons Why I Love You

Day 308: With you the only choice I intend to make whether to buy a waterbed or create a waterbed

Me:
_____

_____

You:
_____

_____

Day 309: The way you ride me like you stole me

Me:

_____

_____

You:

_____

_____

365 Erotic Reasons Why I Love You

Day 310: It drives you crazy when I put on my glasses

Me:

You:

Day 311: The hour-long massage and the message it conveyed

Me:

You:

Day 312: You make porn-stars look like prudish first time virgins

Me:

———————————————

———————————————

You:

———————————————

———————————————

Day 313: You bought the condo because the kitchen was big enough for "activities"

Me:

You:

Day 314: Not even a Caribbean pirate could take control of booty better

Me:

You:

Day 315: Watching you laugh hysterically makes me think of all of the lovely things I could place in your mouth

Me:

You:

Day 316: When I surprise you and take a fistful of happiness

Me:

———————————————

———————————————

You:

———————————————

———————————————

Day 317: The way you melt in my mouth and in my hands

Me:

You:

Day 318: Going to the dentist because of the cavity you gave me

Me:

You:

Day 319: The way your body sways and bends with eagerness is why I can't fathom turning out the lights

Me:

You:

Day 320: You've found creative ways to get rid of the candy the kids brought home from Halloween.

Me:

You:

Day 321: You accepted my challenge to make an X-rated snow angel

Me:

————————————

————————————

You:

————————————

————————————

365 Erotic Reasons Why I Love You

Day 322: Because of you we can never return to that movie theatre

Me:

You:

365 Erotic Reasons Why I Love You

Day 323: The moment after I place my hand on your cheek and slide the hair on your face behind your ear

Me:
_____

_____

You:
_____

_____

Day 324: When we have a night of drinking you ensure that I'm hanging over something before I have a hang over

Me:

You:

Day 325: After that I am knee deep in your closet searching for your cape because you must be a superhero

Me:

You:

365 Erotic Reasons Why I Love You

Day 326: I am thankful that you can never keep your hands off of me

Me:

You:

Day 327: I can't find a reason to use the Love Coupon Book you gave me for Valentine's Day

Me:

You:

Day 328: We rode the motorcycle and never left the driveway

Me:

You:

Day 329: While you were gone you wrote me love letters and decided to wait until you could hold me to read them aloud

Me:

You:

365 Erotic Reasons Why I Love You

Day 330: When you decide to play your instruments in the nude

Me:

You:

Day 331: At the beach watching your body emerge from the water towards me

Me:

You:

Day 332: Serving me breakfast in bed with only a smile

Me:

You:

365 Erotic Reasons Why I Love You

Day 333: The compassion you showed someone in need when you thought I wasn't looking

Me:

You:

Day 334: Watching you crawl to me for mercy though I don't have any to give

Me:

You:

Day 335: How surprised you are when you realize my leg really does reach over there

Me:

You:

365 Erotic Reasons Why I Love You

Day 336: How cute you are when I use your freckles as blueprints to construct bliss

Me:

You:

Day 337: Making me feel like a piece of meat during Shark Week

Me:

You:

Day 338: The goose bumps I get when you walk through the door

Me:

You:

Day 339: How electric everything becomes during that first moment of penetration

Me:

You:

365 Erotic Reasons Why I Love You

Day 340: You bring the classroom to my dorm room

Me:

You:

---

365 Erotic Reasons Why I Love You

Day 341: The thought of having 2 of you nearly puts me in cardiac arrest

Me:

You:

365 Erotic Reasons Why I Love You

Day 342: Because I know you're not done until you lick your fingers and smack your lips

Me:

You:

Day 343: The erotic way you bridge my imagination to my reality

Me:

You:

Day 344: Thanking the heavens that spank proof armor does not exist

Me:

You:

365 Erotic Reasons Why I Love You

Day 345: You're strong enough to apologize

Me:

You:

365 Erotic Reasons Why I Love You

Day 346: Remembering the first time and how you trembled with anticipation

Me:

_____

_____

You:

_____

_____

Day 347: The Kama Sutra has now become a checklist instead of a reference guide

Me:

_____

_____

You:

_____

_____

365 Erotic Reasons Why I Love You

Day 348: That moment where I don't know where my limbs end and yours begin

Me:

You:

Day 349: Happy that whether it's a parking garage, a public pool or dance floor there will be people who are amazed by our sensuality

Me:

You:

Day 350: Creating your potion that includes 1 lb of lewdness, an ounce of curiosity, a pinch of audacity mixed 2 parts passion and 1 part power on high for 365 days a year

Me:

_____

_____

You:

_____

_____

Day 351: How you tortuously drag one finger down my body repeatedly

Me:

You:

Day 352: The way your muscles ache to give me what I desire

Me:

You:

Day 353: Watching the journey of hot slickness pouring from your core

Me:

You:

Day 354: When I have nothing left to give you, you always find more

Me:

You:

Day 355: We both believe that knee and elbow pads should be added to sex catalogues

Me:

You:

Day 356: Your touch allows me the capacity to implode and explode simultaneously

Me:

You:

Day 357: Before you I thought catching lockjaw was an urban myth

Me:

You:

365 Erotic Reasons Why I Love You

Day 358: Though your love is invisible I can still smell and taste it

Me:

You:

365 Erotic Reasons Why I Love You

Day 359: The way you crave my morning dew

Me:

_____

_____

You:

_____

_____

Day 360: Your unexpected kisses that make all my hairs stand on end

Me:
_____

_____

You:
_____

_____

365 Erotic Reasons Why I Love You

Day 361: No matter how bad my day was I know it will all melt away once we're in each other's arms

Me:

You:

365 Erotic Reasons Why I Love You

Day 362. There aren't words to describe what you do to me

Me:

You:

365 Erotic Reasons Why I Love You

Day 363: Your love doesn't come with limits

Me:

You:

Day 364: How your love serves as a lighthouse when I've lost my way

Me:

_____

_____

You:

_____

_____

Day 365: Because you've changed my life

Me:

You:

365 Erotic Reasons Why I Love You

THE END

www.ingramcontent.com/pod-product-compliance
Lightning Source LLC
LaVergne TN
LVHW051541070426
835507LV00021B/2352